Really Happened

Space Stories
that
Really Happened

Andrew Donkin

Illustrated by David Wyatt

Hippo

This book is dedicated to my dad,
who had the good sense to wake me up when I
was five years old and carry me downstairs in a
blanket at three in the morning so that I could watch
Neil Armstrong take his first steps on the moon.
"This is history," he said.
He was right. A.D.

Commonwealth House, 1-19 New Oxford Street,
London WC1A 1NU, UK

A division of Scholastic Ltd
London ~ New York ~ Toronto ~ Sydney ~ Auckland
Mexico City ~ New Delhi ~ Hong Kong

Published in the UK by Scholastic Ltd, 1999

Text copyright © Andrew Donkin, 1999
Illustrations copyright © David Wyatt, 1999

ISBN 0 590 11102 7

All rights reserved
Typeset by Falcon Oast Graphic Art Ltd.
Printed and bound by Bath Press, Bath.

2 4 6 8 10 9 7 5 3 1

The right of Andrew Donkin and David Wyatt to be identified as the
author and illustrator of this work respectively has been asserted by them
in accordance with the Copyright, Designs and Patents Act, 1988.

Contents

Before you begin…

Everybody wants to be an astronaut. At least they did in my school.

Astronauts are heroes. Not because of the risks involved in travelling into the hostile environment of space, but because of the years of hard work and endless training that they have to do before they can get even as far as the launch pad.

This book contains six stories about space. To make them more enjoyable to read, some of the conversations have been made up, but all of the stories really happened. Some of them changed the world.

Everybody wants to be an astronaut.

I did.

I still do.

Andrew Donkin

All Alone in the Night

Star City, Russia
12 April 1961

I had never expected to change the world so much just by flying around it.

When my Vostok rocket left the launch pad I was an unknown test pilot. By the time it returned two hours later, I – Yuri Gagarin – had somehow become the most famous man in the world.

No one had ever flown outside of the

Earth's atmosphere before in the whole of human history and my flight would change for ever the way people thought and felt about their place in the universe. It was the beginning of the space age.

I had never even dreamed about going into space when I was younger, but I had always wanted to fly. I can still remember the exact day that I saw my first ever aeroplane as a child.

It was during the Second World War when two Russian planes suddenly appeared over the horizon engaged in a frantic dog-fight with two enemy German aircraft.

I knew from the moment that I saw those planes weaving and spiralling through the sky that I had to be a pilot. Any kind of pilot.

 Now, as I stood putting on my spacesuit, I realized I was about to become the world's first spaceman.

On the morning of the launch, it took me over an hour to get dressed.

First, the doctors had attached sensors to my chest to record my heartbeat and body temperature during the flight. Then they had helped me put on the white padded pressure suit and finally slipped on the bright orange overall.

All that remained was for me to squeeze on my boots and I was ready.

Through the window I could see the clear blue sky. It looked like the perfect day for a launch. Maybe that was a good omen, I thought to myself.

"You ready to make history then?" said a voice from behind me.

Standing in the doorway was Gherman Titov, my backup pilot in case anything went wrong at the last minute and stopped me from flying. We had got to know each other very well over the last few months.

Gherman and I had both been picked from the Air Force and chosen for Russia's brand-new space programme. Together with four others we had undergone intensive training for over a year, in preparation for the world's maiden space flight.

No one knew how space was going to affect a human. The six of us had all volunteered to be human guinea pigs. We all wanted to be the first person into space despite the obvious risks.

Eventually, the selectors had picked me to take the very first flight. Sometimes I like to think it was because of my flying skills; other times I think it was because I was not very tall and fitted into the Vostok spacecraft better than the others.

The purpose of this mission was to complete one orbit around the globe and to return safely to Earth. No one knew if it could be done.

"You are about to become a great

Russian hero," said Gherman.

"Maybe," I said. "If I get back in one piece."

"No, my friend," said Gherman, with a big grin. "Either way!"

I managed a smile and we headed outside to where the bus was waiting to take both of us to the launch pad.

I knew that Gherman would have given anything to swap places with me and blast off instead and I found myself feeling a little sorry for him. He had trained as hard as I had, but he was going nowhere. At least not today.

Our bus drove slowly across the grey concrete of the base. In the distance loomed the towering shape of the Vostok rocket. Attached to the main body were the four powerful booster rockets that would help blast it into orbit.

The bus pulled up to the launch pad and

I stepped out. Gherman tried to give me a Russian kiss on the cheek for luck, but our helmets banged together loudly instead.

A crowd of workers, technicians and scientists had gathered to wish me well and some of them began to ask me to sign autographs. It was my first taste of how things would be when I got back, my first taste of suddenly being famous.

A technician led me towards the waiting spacecraft and a lift took us up the side of the rocket to the capsule.

"Everything is ready. I'll lower you into the capsule then seal the hatch," said the technician. "God be with you."

I squeezed inside and on to the single seat. There was not a centimetre of spare room anywhere on board. In front of me was a simple control panel. It had some switches and indicator lights, a clock, and a little globe of the Earth that would show the location of my spaceship.

As soon as I was safely in position the technicians slammed shut the hatch.

"Are you receiving me?" said a voice in my earpiece. It was ground control who were based in a huge underground bunker near the launch pad.

"Receiving you loud and clear, control," I answered.

"We are about to begin the 90 minute countdown sequence. Countdown begins in five, four, three, two, one, zero..."

For the next hour and a half, I sat in the cramped capsule while the clock ticked away. Ground control ran numerous equipment checks over and over again.

"Are you getting bored in there?" asked a voice.

"Some music would be nice," I said, only half joking. I didn't feel nervous really, just anxious to get things started and get moving after so much time spent in training.

At last, the clock ticked down to ten minutes, then five, then one.

"Launch control to go position," said a voice.

"Stand by."

At exactly 9:06 a.m., the general in charge of the launch pressed the ignition button in ground control's underground bunker.

"We have ignition."

I felt the rocket begin to sway as the fuel lines were yanked away. The craft began to rumble like an earthquake, then the vibrations got deeper and deeper as the whole ship began to shake with a series of violent tremors.

For just a moment I wondered if the rocket would simply explode on the launch pad in a huge ball of fire.

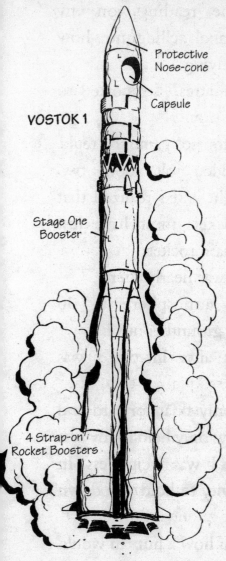

VOSTOK 1

Protective Nose-cone

Capsule

Stage One Booster

4 Strap-on Rocket Boosters

Slowly at first, but then with an ever-growing roar, the rocket began to rise.

The rocket picked up speed and began to fight against the pull of the Earth's gravity – called g-forces. I was pushed down into my seat. As the g-forces reached maximum strength, I could feel the flesh on my face vibrating. Because of the protective nose-cone over the top of the rocket, I could not see out of the window. Instead, I had to watch the readings on my control panel telling me how high I was flying.

"I am at 50,000 metres," I reported to ground control.

"You are right on course," came the reply.

There was a sudden jolt about two minutes into the flight and I realized that the four booster rockets must have just separated from the main rocket.

That meant that I was nearly there.

"Leaving Earth's atmosphere in 30 seconds," announced ground control.

Just nine minutes after lift-off, I was in orbit.

I felt myself suddenly float forward and realized that I was now only held in my seat by the safety straps. I was weightless. In space there is no gravity to hold you down so you just float.

No one had known how a human would

cope with weightlessness. Some of the scientists had even said that it might affect a person's mind and make them go mad. I felt fine.

"Weightlessness has begun," I reported to ground control. "I'm feeling good. Everything's going well."

The nose-cone suddenly detached itself from the top of the ship.

"Nose-cone jettisoned. I can see outside!"

At last I could look out of the window.

"I can see clouds. I can see everything. It's beautiful!" I told ground control.

I had flown many aircraft to great heights as a test pilot, but this was completely different.

Below me, frosted white clouds drifted across the coastline of northern Russia.

The whole globe of the Earth lay spread out before me with its patchwork blues and greens.

I knew that I was the first man ever to see our own planet from space.

I could lift my hand and blot out every other human being in the universe.

"It looks fantastic!" I said, and started to describe what I could see to the people back on the ground.

Vostok was now in orbit, travelling at eight kilometres per second – the fastest speed that a human had ever travelled.

The Earth seemed quiet and peaceful from orbit. There were no noises of cars, or guns, or people arguing. Just the regular and reassuring noises of a spacecraft working well.

I could see
the outlines of familiar
countries. From this height, even
large cities containing millions of people
were no more than grey blobs.

Vostok passed into the dark of the Earth's
shadow and over the half of the planet
where it was night. Over South America I
caught sight of a huge formation of storm
clouds, with their swirling patterns gently
twisting into each other.

I made a note of everything
that I saw on a tape recorder
and mentioned each country as
I passed over it.

"Vostok, you are approaching Africa.
Stand by to fire retro-rockets," ordered
ground control.

"Understood," I answered.

I had been in space for just over an hour,
but it felt like only a few minutes. Already
my flight was nearly over. I wanted to stay
longer. I wanted to go around again.
Suddenly I was sure that man's future lay in
space. I knew that there would be more
launches, more voyages.

As I left Africa behind, the Vostok's
retro-rockets began to fire. Their job was
to slow the spacecraft down, so that it
would begin to fall back to Earth.

"Preparing for re-entry," I said.

I could feel the tiny craft banging against

the upper reaches of the atmosphere. Suddenly it was a very bumpy journey and the craft began spinning around: slowly at first, but then building faster and faster.

I realized something had gone badly wrong.

Just before re-entry, the Vostok craft was supposed to separate into two pieces. The forward silver ball with me inside should have come free of the larger equipment module behind it.

Somehow they had remained attached to each other. One of the cables was still in place, locking the two sections together.

Instead of the silver ball portion

smoothly re-entering the atmosphere, the two parts of the craft were caught together, tumbling over and over each other.

Almost at once I began to hear a crackling sound from the ship itself and I felt the temperature inside the capsule begin to increase.

The main heat shield that was supposed to protect the ship from the incredible heat of re-entry was positioned on one side of the Vostok. Because the craft was spinning around, other less protected areas of the ship were being exposed.

Now I was going to find out how well the chief designer had done his job.

Through the window I could see that the outside of the spacecraft was warming up. A few seconds more and the whole ship was glowing a fiery red colour as it was heated to 3,000 degrees.

I held on tightly as the tiny ship was buffeted around, knowing that if the heat shield failed then I would be burned alive.

Suddenly the craft jolted with a violent lurch. The two parts had finally separated which was good news, but that had made the spinning so bad that I was nearly losing consciousness.

The control panel in front of me seemed to go a hazy grey colour. I had to fight to stay awake. I knew that if I did pass out, I'd never get down alive.

Without warning, I felt the strong g-forces hit me again and I knew that Vostok had made it back into the Earth's atmosphere.

I could see that the outside of the ship was badly burned and charred, but beyond that I could see the welcome sight of blue sky again.

I quickly got ready to exit the ship, gathering together all my notes and my tape recorder.

"Welcome home, Major Gagarin," said ground control. The use of the title "Major" surprised me. It was their way of saying that I'd just earned a promotion.

"Stand by for hatch door release."

A few seconds later, the ship's exit hatch blasted open. There was an enormous rush of wind as it fell away to Earth; then the ejector seat fired me out of the falling craft.

A blast of cold air hit my face as I began to plummet towards the ground far below.

I waited a few seconds to make sure I was clear of the Vostok spaceship, then I pulled the cord on my own smaller parachute.

As I floated back to Earth, I could see my craft below, falling much faster than me. It was now the world's first piece of space junk.

The ground was coming up fast now and I began watching my height carefully, getting ready to roll when I landed. I judged the distance just right and made a safe landing.

I was back.

I had landed in a field and in the distance I could see a puzzled farmer sitting on his tractor watching me.

Ground control would have tracked my descent and have sent out army trucks to search for me. All I had to do was wait for them to find me.

Even now I knew that news of my flight must be spreading around the globe. The world's first spaceman was home. I began to walk towards the man and his tractor.

"Where have you come from?" said the farmer, climbing down.

I smiled. Did I have a tale to tell!

Did you know...?

Astronauts in space

1. When Yuri Gagarin returned to Earth he was guest of honour at a huge parade in Red Square in Moscow. In the months that followed, Gagarin travelled the world, meeting heads of state, including the Queen, and being interviewed by countless newspaper reporters.

Yuri Gagarin is still a much-loved hero today. In Moscow there is a giant steel statue of him that stands a massive 30 metres high.

2. Yuri's backup pilot Gherman Titov

did eventually make it into space. On 6 August 1961 he flew the second manned Vostok flight which lasted 24 hours and completed 17 orbits of the Earth.

3. Today, astronauts always take their passport with them when they travel in space. They never know when they might have to make an emergency landing in another country on the way down.

4. Astronauts grow when they go into space. Because there is no gravity pulling them down, the bones in a person's back move apart a little. The result is that a person is five centimetres taller in space than they are on the ground.

5. During Apollo 8, Frank Borman suffered from space sickness and threw up. Unfortunately not everything went into his sickbag. Some of it got away in the zero gravity and Borman had to float after it to try and catch it – one of the many everyday hazards of life for an astronaut.

6. In October 1998, John Glenn became the oldest person ever to go into space, when he blasted off at the age of 77. His job was to study the effects of spaceflight on the human body, and involved him swallowing a thermometer in a capsule so that doctors could record his temperature while he slept.

Rescue and Repair

Shuttle Mission 11: Earth orbit
April 1984

The sleek white shape of the shuttle cut gracefully through the darkness of space, closing in on its target.

With a wingspan of 24 metres and a body length of 38 metres, the space shuttle was the world's first reusable spacecraft.

It blasted off like a normal rocket, behaved like a spaceship while in orbit, then re-entered the atmosphere to glide down to Earth and land like a plane.

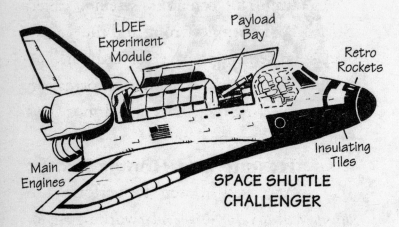

LDEF Experiment Module

Payload Bay

Retro Rockets

Main Engines

Insulating Tiles

SPACE SHUTTLE CHALLENGER

"How much longer?" asked George Nelson, impatiently.

"Five minutes, maybe ten," said Robert Crippen, the shuttle's commander.

The two astronauts floated in the zero gravity looking out through the ship's main window. Their attention was focused on a tiny black dot, far away in the distance.

"Doesn't look like 200 million dollars, does it?" said Crippen, pointing at the distant object.

"Not from here anyway," smiled Nelson.

An important scientific satellite called Solar Max had gone wrong and the shuttle had been sent into space to repair it. The satellite was used to gather information about the sun, but its control box had developed a major fault.

George Nelson was the Mission Specialist that NASA had chosen to perform the space walk to get Solar Max working again.

"You know the plan," said Crippen. "Get to the satellite as quickly, but safely, as you can. Bring it back to the shuttle for repairs, then relaunch it."

No one had ever attempted to repair a satellite in space before. But with satellites becoming more and more expensive, repairing them made better sense than launching new ones.

As the two men watched, the

distant black dot was getting bigger.

"We're closing in," said Crippen.

Up on the shuttle's flight deck, the pilot Francis Scobee was carefully manoeuvring the ship nearer and nearer the crippled satellite.

"Closing in on target," said Scobee.

They were close enough now for the men to get a good view. The satellite was a rectangular shape with two large solar panels extending from its sides.

"We're now 60 metres from the satellite," said Scobee. "This is as close as I can take us."

"I'll go and get suited up," said Nelson, floating towards the shuttle's spacelab.

When Nelson had finished putting on his spacesuit, Crippen lowered a space helmet over Nelson's head and clicked it into place.

To his surprise, Nelson realized that he was floating inside the suit, his head sometimes rising to bob against the top of the helmet.

"How does it feel?" asked Crippen.

"Like I just put on three stones in blubber," smiled Nelson, looking down at the bulky spacesuit.

"Well, don't worry. Here's the best part," said Crippen, pointing towards a strange looking device waiting near the airlock.

 "Your MMU."

The letters "MMU" stood for Manned Manoeuvring Unit. It

was NASA's newest invention.

Until recently an astronaut had to be attached to his spaceship by a line or cable to stop them floating away. The MMU had changed all that.

The unit looked rather like a high-tech armchair and had 24 tiny thrusters that controlled its exact direction and speed. It was like a space-age jet pack and it turned an astronaut into a mini-spaceship.

The MMU had a maximum speed of 20 metres per second and had cost nine million dollars to build.

"Remember," warned Crippen, "don't waste fuel by flying too far from the ship. And most important of all, don't hit anything. I mean anything. Even a low speed collision could rip a hole in your spacesuit."

He gave Nelson a big grin.

"Ready?"

"As I'll ever be," said Nelson.

He stepped inside the ship's airlock and Crippen slammed it firmly shut behind him.

"Good luck," said Crippen, over their radio link.

"Opening outer airlock door now," reported Nelson, giving it a hard push.

He moved to the edge of the airlock.

It was an odd feeling.

Until now, George Nelson had always been on Earth or inside a spaceship, but here he was, about to go into space completely unattached to anybody or anything.

"I'm stepping out."

Nelson pushed himself forward and floated through the outer door of the airlock. He was now alone, floating freely in orbit around the Earth.

Nelson could see the shape of the Solar Max satellite ahead of him, and behind it the huge globe of the Earth.

On the edge of the Earth, he could see the blackness of space becoming the dark purple and then the sky blue of the atmosphere.

"Nelson, do you read me?" asked Crippen, over the radio.

Nelson realized he must have been sightseeing a bit too long.

"Roger, Commander. Beginning test."

Now that Nelson was clear of the ship, he could begin to use the MMU.

He had to make sure he could control his own movements before he tried to dock with the satellite.

Nelson gently squeezed the left-hand joystick and felt himself being propelled forward.

"This thing's working great," he said, happily.

Nelson flew above the shuttle and looked down. It was a strange sight, being able to look down at your own ship as it travelled through space. The cargo bay doors were open. He could see the ship's robot arm tucked away as well as the repair station waiting for the satellite.

Nelson began practising flying the MMU. He was amazed by what it could do. He could move, turn, even somersault if he wanted to.

"I'm ready to attempt docking with Solar Max," announced Nelson after the test was over.

"Understood. Good luck," responded Crippen.

Nelson used the MMU thrusters to turn around and slowly headed towards Solar Max. He had to judge his speed very carefully, or he could overshoot his target.

"I'm moving into range now," reported Nelson. His eyes were fixed intently on the satellite.

Adjusting his control stick, Nelson flew under the main body of the satellite, carefully avoiding the solar panels on both sides.

Nelson almost came to a complete stop, then began edging nearer and nearer. He had to be very careful. If he banged into Solar Max, he could send it spinning wildly out of its orbit and out of control for ever.

"I am at the satellite now. About to make contact."

Nelson was very close now and let himself drift the last few metres towards the Solar Max.

"Contact. I am on the satellite," announced Nelson.

The plan was for Nelson to latch himself on by using a special docking device. Then to use the MMU to move the satellite towards the space shuttle.

"Latching on now," said Nelson.

He lined up the docking device on the MMU and pushed it forward.

Nothing happened.

"I'm trying again." He backed the docking sections apart and then brought them together again. Still nothing happened.

Nelson tried for a third time. Then a fourth. The units would not link up with each other as they should have. Something was wrong.

He could not dock with the satellite.

"It's not working, Commander," reported Nelson, disappointed. "I can't get it to dock."

Nelson knew that this was a real problem. They might even have to abandon the satellite rescue altogether. He checked his watch: his oxygen supply was going fast.

Nelson knew that he could not simply grab the satellite because he might cause it to spin dangerously.

What else could they do? Nelson was desperate for his mission to succeed. If he didn't think of something fast, this whole trip was going to be a very expensive failure.

He looked around him. On Earth he would have had all sorts of options, but up here there was just him and the shuttle.

The shuttle? Its payload doors were open and Nelson again caught sight of the long robot arm stored in the cargo bay.

The robot arm or RMS (Remote Manipulator System) was 15 metres long and was, before the invention of the MMU, used as a safety platform for astronauts as they worked outside in space.

Maybe it could be used another way?

"Nelson to shuttle. I've got an idea," said the astronaut. "How about using the robot arm to snatch the satellite out of orbit? I'll stay out here and act as your guide. I'll keep close to the satellite and let you know what's happening."

It was dangerous, but it made sense.

"Let's see what the boys downstairs have to say," said Commander Crippen as he went away to talk to Mission Control.

He came back on the radio link a few minutes later. "Let's do it, but be careful. Mission Control are having kittens down there. We'll take it nice and slow. You guide us in."

Using the automatic controls in the shuttle, Crippen brought the robot arm to life and extended it to its full length of 15 metres.

"Keep coming," said Nelson. "Further. Further. Open the grip on the end of the arm."

Nelson used the MMU to get himself exactly between the robot arm and the satellite.

"Keep coming forward. More. Slowly. Just a bit more."

Suddenly the arm jerked forward just missing the lower part of the satellite. Nelson knew that if the arm hit the satellite it would be very dangerous, perhaps even fatal for him.

A spinning satellite that was pushed towards him could rip his spacesuit to shreds or even worse, crash into the shuttle itself.

"You've gone too far. Move it back," said Nelson, calmly.

Inside the shuttle, Crippen worked the controls and reversed the arm.

"Try again," said Nelson, as Crippen edged the arm forward once more.

"OK. Open gripping mechanism and stand by," ordered Nelson.

The end of the arm was now perfectly over the bottom of Solar Max.

"Close the grip!" said Nelson, suddenly.

The grip snapped shut.

"You've got it!" said Nelson.

They had hooked their satellite.

The arm began to pull the satellite towards the shuttle with Nelson following behind using his MMU. He knew the most difficult part of the mission was just beginning.

"Satellite in cargo bay," announced Nelson, as he locked it down.

 "Now I can get to work."

Nelson's first task was to take off one of the satellite's

side panels so that he could see inside it.

The worst problem now was Nelson's own spacesuit. The bulky material of his gloves made hand movements very difficult. It was like trying to thread a needle wearing mittens.

Nelson could feel himself getting hotter and hotter inside his suit and had to concentrate hard on the task at hand.

With the panel removed, Nelson located the broken control box. He pulled it out and carefully eased the new box into place.

"I'm replacing the outer panel," said Nelson, beginning to put it back into place.

"We're ready for relaunch," said Nelson when he was finished.

Crippen controlled the robot arm as it lifted the satellite clear of the shuttle's bay doors.

It was vital that they release the satellite without putting it into a spin which could send it off course.

Nelson floated near the robot arm, watching the operation closely.

"Stand by for release. Five, four, three, two, one, release," he said, counting down his commander.

The grip on the end of the robot arm opened quickly and cleanly. The arm withdrew, folding neatly back into the shuttle's cargo bay.

"Get yourself back in here," ordered Crippen.

With a burst of thruster fire, Nelson flew towards the ship's airlock. The MMU controls seemed second nature to him now.

"Looking good, shuttle. How does it read?" said Nelson anxiously.

He knew that this was the moment of truth. Was the satellite working again?

"Mission Control are getting the first readings," said Crippen. "Looks like it's back in business."

"Yes!" said Nelson.

As he headed back towards the shuttle, Nelson smiled to himself. He was the first repairman ever to make a house call in orbit.

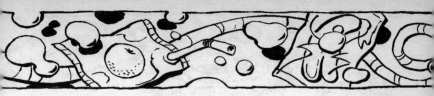

Did you know...?

Life in space

1. Spacesuits cost a cosmic two million pounds each to make. However, they are worth it. If an astronaut went for a space walk without a suit, his blood would boil and his body would inflate like a balloon.

2. One unexpected side-effect of spending time in space is that astronauts often lose their sense of taste. After a week or so even their favourite food ends up tasting like newspaper.

3. To keep them fit, astronauts planning lengthy stays in space must work out for about two hours each day of their space flight

otherwise their muscles would waste away.

4. Astronauts have three meals a day, but have to choose exactly what they want to eat before they blast off. In the early days, astronauts ate straight from containers shaped like toothpaste tubes. Today the selection and quality of foods available is much greater.

5. On board the American space shuttle, astronauts get a night's rest in sleeping-bags fixed on to the shuttle's walls to prevent the astronauts floating about during the night.

6. Going to the toilet in space is always a tricky business for any astronaut. Space toilets work by using a system of flowing air to make up for the lack of gravity.

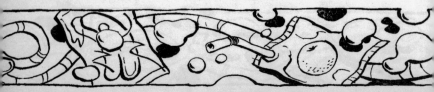

The Martians are Coming!

New Jersey, USA
30 October 1938

What I want to tell you about happened one Hallowe'en when a lot of people, my father included, went a bit crazy.

It was the night when we all nearly fell victim to hideous tentacled monsters from Mars and we only just managed to escape with our lives.

It all happened on a dark Sunday

evening in 1938 — which must seem about a million years ago to you today.

It was 30 October, the night before Hallowe'en, and because it was a weekend there were kids out in their costumes already trick-or-treating.

From my bedroom window I could see Frankenstein's monster, Dracula, and three wolfmen at the door of Mrs Berman's house across the street.

In her front window was a huge pumpkin with a candle burning inside. The eyes had been cut so that it had a really mean look, like they were staring straight at you.

The first sign that anything unusual was up was when Dad called me to come downstairs. I thought that he wanted me to put out the trash, so naturally I ignored him.

I got out the new issue of *Amazing Stories* and settled down for a quiet read. According to my father I "always had my head stuck in some book more than what was good for me".

My bedroom door suddenly flew open and there was Dad. I thought I was in real trouble, but he just said, "Hey, get down here," and then disappeared.

Downstairs, Mum and Dad were sitting hunched by the radio set.

In those days nearly all our news came from the radio. Dad said that it was more reliable than the newspapers and it was always where we heard the important news first.

At the moment it sounded like they were listening to some sappy dance band.

"There's something happening at Grover's Mill," said Dad.

"What do you mean?"

"You're interested in all that space stuff, aren't you?" asked Dad.

I was a bit puzzled, but I knew it had to be important if it was on the radio news.

"We were listening to Ramon Raquello and his dance band, but they started interrupting him with special announcements. Some professor guy at Princeton Observatory saw three blue flashes on the surface of Mars. Then they said that some kind of meteorite had landed at Grover's Mill, New Jersey."

"That's only half an hour's drive away," I said.

"Twenty minutes in the new car," said Dad, proudly.

Space stuff *was* kind of a hobby of mine and I really wanted to know if a meteorite had landed.

Meteorites are pieces of rock that float through space and occasionally hit the Earth. If this was one, it was very unusual and I *had* to see it.

Suddenly the sappy dance music faded away and the announcer said in a serious voice, "We interrupt this programme again to bring you a special bulletin."

I sat with Mum and Dad and the three of us huddled around our Zenith radio set, hanging on the announcer's every word.

Their radio reporter, someone called Carl Phillips, had just arrived at the scene in Grover's Mill.

"See I told you it was Grover's Mill," said Dad triumphantly, like no one had believed him.

The reporter began describing the

scene, painting a picture with his words.

In front of him was a huge pit that had been carved out of part of a farmer's field. In the pit, half hidden and half visible, was a huge silver cylinder. Steam rose from where the metal had been heated up by its impact. Its sides were rounded and smooth.

It didn't sound like a meteorite to me.

"Could be those Japanese," said Dad, but no one was listening to him. I couldn't believe that all this was happening just a few kilometres away.

The reporter described how a large crowd was starting to gather around the pit.

"Can we go down there too, Dad?"

"Maybe."

"Remember, tomorrow is a school day," added Mum, unhelpfully.

Back at Grover's Mill, there were reports of a strange grating sound coming from inside the cylinder. The reporter took his microphone nearer the object to capture the sound.

We all leaned towards the radio set to listen even more carefully.

"What is going on?" asked Mum.

"Sssssh," said Dad.

"The top of the cylinder is beginning to rotate and unscrew. It must be hollow," reported the voice of Carl Phillips.

This was exciting. What was going to be inside?

Dad put his hand on my back and deliberately made me jump.

"Get off!"

"It is Hallowe'en, you know," he smiled.

There was a whole heap of shouting and noise from the crowd. Phillips moved closer for a better view.

"Something is crawling out of the cylinder. It's some kind of creature. It's ugly. Its glistening black body is about the size of a large bear. It's got tentacles, like grey snakes, coming out of its sides."

"Oh my Lord," whispered Mum.

"And a face. A horrible face with black gleaming eyes and saliva dripping from its mouth," said the voice of Carl Phillips, sounding more and more revolted.

"Sounds like one of your bug-eyed monsters," said Dad, nodding at the copy of *Amazing Stories* still in my hand.

The crowd around the pit began to panic, and then run and the reporter had to go off the air.

He was replaced by the sound of someone playing the piano – what always happened when they needed to fill in time.

"I wonder if Harvey's listening to this?" said Dad. Harvey was Dad's best friend.

He lived next door to us.

Carl Phillips came back on the air and described how the pit was now being surrounded on all sides by the police.

I wondered how they would arrest the creatures. Would they be able to put handcuffs on their tentacles?

"Something's rising out of the pit. Some kind of device. Oh my word! It's shooting out a wall of flame!" said Phillips, with fear rising in his voice.

In the background, we could hear the sound of men screaming. Then the broadcast was suddenly cut off.

In our small front room, no one spoke.

We sat in silence as the piano music came back on.

 A few moments later someone called General Montgomery Smith came on to the air and declared a state of emergency in the area around Grover's Mill.

He sounded grim and somehow hopeless.

There was chaos and confusion at the landing site, but the radio people had tracked down someone who described what had happened.

The crowd around the pit had been attacked by a terrible weapon belonging to the creatures.

The reporter called the weapon a "Heat-Ray" and something clicked in the back of my mind, but I didn't know what. Not yet anyway.

"Maybe...?" said Mum.

"Maybe we ought to get out of here," said Dad, finishing her thought.

"They're calling in the Army. This is like a war or something."

Another voice on the radio told us that 7,000 troops were now surrounding the pit. Suddenly things seemed to be under control again.

"What kind of creatures are they?" said Mum, to no one in particular.

"Martians," I whispered, before I could stop myself.

"Kid's right. Probably damn Martians," agreed Dad, like he was suddenly an expert on galactic warfare.

Back at the pit, another radio

reporter described the banging and drilling noises that were now coming from the creatures' dark lair.

"Hey, maybe they're trying to repair their rocket ship," said Dad.

It was a pretty smart idea, especially coming from Dad, but I didn't think he was right.

"Then why not ask for help?" I said. "Why attack people with a Heat-Ray?"

There was that word again – "Heat-Ray".

The voice of the man now in charge, Captain Lansing, began speaking, reassuring listeners that the situation was under control.

The Army had completely surrounded the pit and the strange creatures seemed happy enough to hide away inside.

The Captain described the Army's spotlights moving around. Every now and then one of the lights would pick out something wet and glistening in the deep darkness of the pit.

The soldiers closed in, getting ready to attack.

"This'll teach them a lesson for using that Heat-Ray," grinned Dad. "Give them a taste of their own medicine."

As the troops advanced, Captain Lansing saw something moving about in the pit. A huge silver shape suddenly rose out of the gloom.

It was some kind of three-legged tripod machine – and inside was one of the creatures.

That's what the banging had been. They'd been building some kind of machine.

Without warning, Captain Lansing's voice was cut off.

For a few seconds we were left listening to the worst sound I have ever heard on the radio.

Silence.

The studio announcer finally returned and said that the creatures had turned their deadly Heat-Ray on the soldiers.

Many of the troops had been crushed to death under the massive metal feet of the tripod machine. Others had simply been burned to a cinder by the Heat-Ray.

It was a disaster.

Earth was being invaded by alien creatures, probably Martians, and no one, not even the Army, could stop them.

"That's it. We're getting out of here,"

said Dad. "Ellen, get some food together and some warm clothes. I'll get the car out of the garage. We're driving west as fast as we can go."

"What shall I do?" I said.

"Just get ready and wait for... No, you go next door and tell Harvey what's happened. They might not even know," ordered Dad.

I ran upstairs like I had a rocket on my back and put on my coat and shoes.

I ducked under the fence that separated our front yards and rang their bell.

As I waited I could see Dad frantically backing the car out of the garage. He left the engine running and ran back inside the house.

The front door finally opened and there was Mr Pekar.

"It's not Hallowe'en until tomorrow," he said.

"I know, sir. You see the thing of it is..."

My voice kind of faded out.

Now that I had to explain it
to someone else it sounded
kind of, well, stupid.

"You see we were listening to the radio
and I don't know if you know or not, but,
well, Grover's Mill is being invaded by
Martians," I explained.

"Martians, huh?"

I told Mr Pekar the whole story.

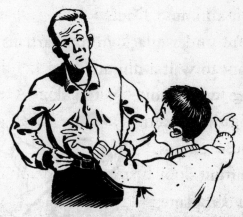

"You mean just like in *The War of the
Worlds*?" he said when I'd finished.

Now I remembered.

That's where "Heat-Ray" came from. *The War of the Worlds* was a book by H.G. Wells and it had a story just like what was happening in Grover's Mill.

The book was set in England ages ago, but the story was almost the same.

I raced back to tell Dad. Maybe we weren't being invaded after all.

"We're ready. Get in the car."

"Wait a minute, Dad."

"We're under attack from Martians and you want to wait a minute!"

There was a noise in the sky. A small dot of light moved against the clouds.

It was just a normal aeroplane, but Dad's eyes widened with sheer and total panic.

"It's them!"

Dad ducked down behind the car. Then he yelled at me to get in again so I slid on to the rear seat.

"Hurry up," said Mum.

Dad screeched away really fast and we headed into the night.

I was sitting on something hard. It turned out to be 15 tins of corned beef.

As we raced down the street, we saw a group of people walking casually along.

"Those poor fools. They've got no idea," said Dad, shaking his head.

He put down his window and bellowed at the very top of his voice, "The Martians are coming! The Martians are coming!"

One of the girls in the group laughed and gave him a friendly wave.

Dad was driving like a maniac now and I had to shout just to make myself heard over the noise of the engine.

"Dad, I think that the Heat-Ray thing and the tripod idea come from a book called *The War of the Worlds*."

"You do, huh? I always said those crazy books of yours would lead to trouble one day. You think that's where the real Martians got their idea to invade Earth?" said Dad.

He still didn't get it.

I was about to have another go at explaining it to him when we were nearly all killed.

Dad had turned on to the main freeway and had to swerve to avoid hitting another car.

Instead of the usual orderly traffic on the road, it looked and sounded more like a racetrack.

There were hundreds of cars, all jam-packed with people and all hurtling along at top speed. From the look of terror on the drivers' faces, I guessed that they were fleeing from the Martians as well.

I have to admit, Dad was a pretty good driver. He skilfully weaved between the speeding cars and we overtook dozens of them.

"Watch it, buddy!" shouted Dad, just skidding in front of a red sports car and stealing its place.

We all raced down the freeway for at least ten minutes at top speed. All of us heading for the Brandford Bridge that led to the safety of the next county.

As we neared the bridge, Dad suddenly had to slam on the brakes.

Ahead of us was a huge traffic jam of cars. Walking in between the stuck cars were policemen. Dozens of blue-uniformed policemen.

"There is no need to panic! There is no Martian invasion! Please stop your cars and turn off your engines!" shouted the policeman nearest us.

"The radio reports were only a hoax broadcast. I repeat, there is no Martian invasion!"

The whole thing had been just a radio play by Orson Welles and his Mercury Theatre. A modern version of H.G. Wells's *The War of the Worlds* performed like a series of real radio news reports.

It was just a bunch of actors messing around on Hallowe'en.

Dad was not amused.

"Why, those no good bunch of phonies," he said, among other more colourful descriptions of them.

Mum and Dad had missed the start of the broadcast and thought that it was the real thing.

They were not alone.

Hundreds of other listeners had also been fooled. Some had fled their homes, others had

77

spent the night hiding in their
cellars with shotguns.

Orson Welles later described the
broadcast as "the Mercury Theatre's own
radio version of dressing up in a sheet and
jumping out of a bush and saying 'Boo!'"

The radio play had been written by
Howard Koch and the whole evening
became known as "the night that panicked
America".

It took most of the night to clear that traffic
jam. I sat in the back of the car eating corned
beef till midnight. It was the best time.

In the end, the very end, even Dad
managed a smile.

Looking back now, it might seem like we
were fooled pretty easily – but things were
different then. We really relied on the radio

news and believed everything it
told us. Even about the Martians.

Harvey, next door, never let

my father forget about the invasion and for years afterwards no one could mention the name of Orson Welles in our house for fear of what would happen.

I'll never forget that night. I'll never forget the taste of corned beef at midnight, stuck in the middle of a freeway.

Most of all I'll never forget my father.

I can still see him, gripping the steering wheel of our car and driving like a madman.

Doing everything he could to save us, his family, from the terrible snakelike tentacles of the advancing Martians.

Did you know...?

Our solar system

1. Our solar system includes not only the nine planets, Mercury, Venus, Earth, Mars, Jupiter, Saturn, Uranus, Neptune and Pluto, but dozens of comets and thousands of asteroids as well.

2. "Shooting stars" are not really stars at all. They are pieces of space rock ("meteorites") burning up as they hit the Earth's atmosphere. Many scientists think that a large meteorite hitting the Earth was what helped kill the dinosaurs.

3. The largest volcano in the whole solar

system is on the red planet Mars. It is called Olympus Mons and is ten times as huge as the biggest Earth volcano.

4. There was a collision in our own solar system in 1994. A comet named Shoemaker–Levy smashed into the planet Jupiter causing huge explosions in its atmosphere.

5. The Great Red Spot on Jupiter is really a giant storm – like a hurricane on Earth. It must have been going on for a long time because it was first seen over 300 years ago.

6. The tiny planet of Pluto takes 248 Earth years to go around the sun just once.

7. An "eclipse" of the sun happens when the moon moves directly in front of the sun and blocks off its light for a few minutes. In ancient China, eclipses were believed to be caused by a giant dragon trying to eat the sun.

Unlucky 13

Cape Kennedy, Florida, USA
2:13 p.m., 11 April 1970

Jim Lovell felt the g-forces jolt him back into his seat as the rocket's engines kicked into life.

"Apollo 13, you are go," said a voice from Mission Control in Houston.

One hundred metres underneath Jim Lovell, the giant rocket blasted out heat and fire, burning the launch pad black.

Sitting next to Lovell, Fred Haise and Jack Swigert felt the powerful engines send vibrations though the entire ship as it slowly began to rise. For a long moment it felt like they were sitting on top of the largest firework in the world.

"We have lift-off!" said a happy voice from Mission Control.

Apollo 13 left the launch pad behind and headed upwards.

"Next stop, the moon," said Lovell, checking the control panel in front of him.

"That was a real bumpy lift-off," said Haise.

"The best ones always are," winked Lovell.

Jim Lovell, the commander of Apollo 13, had flown in space three times before. This, however, was the mission he had worked towards all his life – a voyage to the moon. In just a few days, he would walk on the surface of another world.

"Apollo 13, you are looking good," reported Mission Control as the craft climbed upwards, speeding quickly towards Earth orbit.

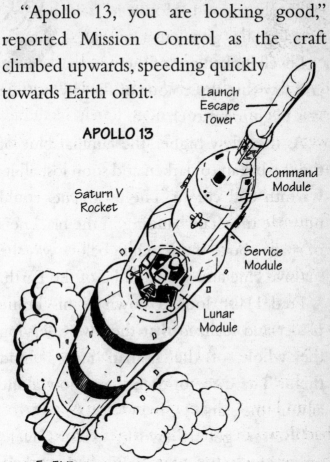

APOLLO 13

Launch Escape Tower

Command Module

Saturn V Rocket

Service Module

Lunar Module

5x F1 Engines

Lovell knew that back at Mission Control every last detail of their flight path was being carefully studied.

"Feeling good, Houston," said Lovell. "She's giving us a fine ride."

Lovell looked out of the window and saw that the colour of the sky outside was beginning to change.

As they flew higher, the familiar blue of the sky began to darken and soon lost all its warmth and colour. The astronauts could now see tiny stars hanging in the blackness of space above them, while below was the massive blue and white globe of the Earth.

Fred Haise looked down at his home planet and realized that they were leaving the whole of the human race behind them. The three of them were now alone among the stars.

"Better get to work," said Lovell, unbuckling his seat-belt. Immediately he began to float upwards towards the ceiling. He gave himself a little shove and spun around on the spot.

Fred Haise had been so busy looking out of the window he hadn't realized that they were now weightless. He undid his belt and floated up too.

Lovell gave himself a push and floated gracefully across the cabin like Superman flying in slow motion. There was no doubt about it, zero gravity was fun.

"Gentlemen," said Lovell, with a big grin, "welcome to outer space."

Jim Lovell was enjoying himself. It was now two days since blast-off and he was giving the television audience at home a tour of the spacecraft.

"And finally, this is where we keep the food," explained Lovell, pointing to a packet of hot dogs in the ship's food store.

"We've just about finished our guided tour," said Lovell with a wave. "So this is the crew of Apollo 13 signing off for the night."

With the TV show over, Jim Lovell and Fred Haise began putting the equipment away.

"That seemed to go OK. Maybe they'll give us our own TV show when we get back to Earth," said Lovell.

"Here, catch," said Haise, giving the camera a push towards Lovell.

It floated gently towards him as if it were suspended on invisible wires. Lovell caught the camera and switched it off.

Suddenly there was a loud bang from the side of the spacecraft.

The two astronauts froze with horror.

Around them the metal walls of their ship buckled and strained. The two astronauts felt the ship jolt from its course and begin to sway from side to side.

"Was that a meteor hit?" asked Haise, his face white with worry.

"If we'd got hit by a meteor, I don't think we'd still be around to discuss it," said Lovell bluntly.

Lovell and Haise raced towards the Command area of the ship where Swigert was already trying to find out what had happened.

"Looks bad," said Swigert quietly.

Never in his life had Lovell seen so many warning lights and alarms going off at the same time.

"Houston, we have a problem," reported Lovell to Mission Control.

"We're trying to work out what has happened," replied Mission Control. "You'll know as soon as we do."

All astronauts go through years of training to prepare them for emergencies in space, but Lovell had never expected anything like this.

Apollo 13 was in the middle of a huge power failure and no one could tell them why.

The lights inside the ship flickered on and off, plunging them into darkness every other second.

Lovell knew that if anything went badly wrong they would

have to forget about the moon landing. As the power level continued to drop, Lovell's chance of walking on the moon was disappearing before his very eyes.

"We're still losing power," said Swigert, as the craft continued to jolt from left to right.

Lovell glanced out of the side window and could hardly believe what he saw.

"Looks like we've got a leak," he said, remembering his training and trying to stay calm.

The others looked out to see that a huge jet of gas was escaping from the side of the ship.

"One of the oxygen tanks must have exploded," said Lovell. "It's still spraying out into space."

Lovell knew now that their situation was much worse than he had first thought.

This was not something they could possibly repair. Not only was a moon landing completely out of the question, but, Lovell realized, they might not even make it back to Earth.

If Apollo 13 kept losing power, the three astronauts would find themselves trapped inside a dead spaceship on a one-way trip to the moon.

During the next few hours, Jim Lovell and his crew used their time finding out exactly what their situation was. It was bad, but not hopeless.

The most important thing they had to do was get Apollo 13 back on course for Earth.

The explosion had been caused by an electrical fault in one of the oxygen tanks. Ever since the accident, Lovell had found himself having to fight for control of the spacecraft.

The gas still escaping made the ship roll from side to side.

"How's it going?" said Swigert, checking up on Lovell's progress.

"The gas leak is really unbalancing her," said Lovell. "This is going to be harder than we thought."

"We've just shut down the main computer to save power," said Swigert.

"Then how are we going to make sure we're on the right course?" asked Lovell, with a frown.

"Mission Control says we'll have to do the calculations ourselves instead of using the computer. There's just not enough power left to keep it switched on."

"Great," said Lovell, through gritted teeth. It was taking all his concentration just to fly the damaged spacecraft.

It took the astronauts over an hour to complete the calculations and work out what course change was needed to make them head for home again.

They prepared to fire up the engines for a course changing burn. It was a long and nerve-racking job.

"Let's take our time and do it right," said Haise, who knew that this change to their flight path would make or break their chances of getting home.

"Ready when you are, Jim," nodded Swigert to his commander.

To help keep himself calm, Lovell thought of all the years of training that they had been through. He told himself that this was just another exercise.

Lovell reached his hand slowly towards the engine control, knowing that all their lives depended on the next few seconds.

"Here we go, 3, 2, 1, fire..."

The three astronauts felt the engines fire and the ship change course. After exactly 21 seconds – and not a second more or a second less – Lovell shut off the engine again.

"How are we doing, Houston?" asked Haise, nervously.

The astronauts sat in silence as they waited to hear Mission Control's verdict. Finally, the answer came.

"Flight path looks good, 13. You're bang on course."

At last something had gone right.

They had put Apollo 13 back on course for Earth. Their fastest way home was to send the ship around the far side of the moon and then let it swing back towards Earth.

They were on target, but from now on air, food, water, and most of all electrical power had to be used very carefully. Otherwise they would run out before they got home.

As the spacecraft passed over the dark side of the moon, the three astronauts gazed down on a landscape seen by only a dozen other humans. Incredible craters and huge mountain ranges littered the lunar surface.

The men were seeing an amazing new world just waiting to be explored, but they could only feel sadness.

If it wasn't for the explosion, Lovell and Haise would be down there right now, exploring it for themselves. They both knew they had missed the chance of a lifetime.

Apollo 13 continued on its journey around the moon, then began to pick up speed as it started the return flight to Earth.

To save what little power the ship had left, the astronauts had already turned off most of the systems. Not just the

computers, but the heating
system as well.

"It's going to get real chilly in
here," said Lovell, as he and Haise settled
down for the night wrapped in blankets.

Lovell and his crew had had almost no
rest since the explosion. Following Mission
Control's advice, they had decided to take
it in turns to try and get some sleep.

It wasn't easy, but eventually they drifted
off. By the time the two astronauts woke up,
it was so cold in the cabin that they could
see their own breath as clouds of mist.

Lovell and Haise floated towards Jack
Swigert who was still sitting at the controls.

In front of Swigert was a pile of strange
objects. Lovell could see a roll of sticky
tape, a plastic bottle, the cover of a book
and a storage bag.

"What are those for?" asked Lovell,
puzzled.

Swigert smiled grimly.

"If we don't do something Mission Control says we're going to run out of fresh air. I've got these things together because we have to make an air purifier to keep the air in the ship fresh," said Swigert.

The astronauts sat down and began to listen to the instructions from Earth. If they didn't get this right they wouldn't be able to breathe for much longer.

Mission Control had worked out how they could build what they needed out of bits and pieces they would have lying around the spacecraft.

"We'll tell you how to do it one step at a time," said Mission Control, patiently.

Making the air purifier took over an hour of careful work.

NASA had the scientific know-how to put a man on the moon, but today the lives of three astronauts depended on the careful use of a roll of sticky tape.

When the device was finished, the men carefully fixed it into position over the air supply pipe. Lovell watched as the oxygen reading in the ship got back to normal.

"We must have got it right. It's working OK," he said with relief.

With that job done, the astronauts could all try and grab a little more rest. They huddled together for warmth, desperately trying to keep out the cold of space.

They were all suffering from the damp and cold conditions in the ship. Particularly Fred Haise who was coming down with a bad chill. Lovell was worried about him and kept a close eye on his condition.

To get them home as fast as possible, Mission Control decided to use the engines one more time. With the computer to help them, this would have been a simple task, but there was not enough power left to switch it on.

To fire the engine correctly would take all three astronauts. Jim Lovell steered the ship, while Fred Haise saw that they were headed in the right direction. Jack Swigert used a clock to make sure the engines were fired for exactly 14 seconds.

Like everything else since the accident, it was perfect teamwork.

"That was a wonderful engine burn, gentlemen, thank you," said Mission Control, after they had had time to track the craft's new speed.

By now the three crewmates had come to rely and trust each other like few Apollo crews before them. No other team of astronauts had faced death together as they had.

Lovell looked out of the window and saw the welcoming globe of the Earth becoming larger with every passing hour.

"There she is, and she looks beautiful," he said, quietly.

Apollo 13 was nearly home, but one more gamble lay ahead.

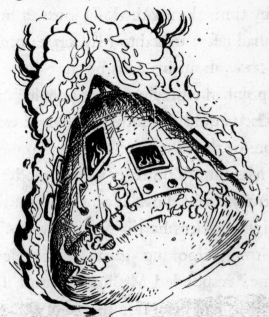

To survive the heat of re-entering the Earth's atmosphere the underside of their ship was covered with a special heat shield. No one knew if the heat shield on Apollo 13 had been damaged by the explosion or not.

If it was broken or even cracked, then they and the ship would simply burn up.

Lovell had thought about the heat shield many times during the long journey home. He had never talked to Mission Control or his crew about his fears because there was no point in worrying other people.

They could do nothing about it except hope for the best.

"Mission Control, we're ready for re-entry," said Lovell, as the ship raced straight towards Earth.

"You're looking great, 13. Welcome home," responded Mission Control. Their scientists had been thinking about the heat shield as well and, like Lovell, all they could do was wait and pray.

"Thanks for all your help, Houston. We'll see you on the other side," said Jack Swigert.

Then Apollo 13 was gone.

The ship disappeared into the two minutes of radio blackout that always occurred during re-entry into the Earth's atmosphere.

Mission Control waited in silence. Each man alone with his own thoughts. Each second seemed to last an hour.

The main clock ticked away one full minute.

Then another.

Apollo 13 should have been out of the blackout by now.

"This is Mission Control, do you read me, Apollo 13?" said a hopeful voice.

There was no reply.

No answer.

"This is Mission Control, do you read us, 13?" said the voice again.

Still no answer.

Then there was an electrifying

crackle and Jim Lovell's voice suddenly burst through the airwaves.

"Mission Control, looks like we made it. We're home!"

Every last person in Mission Control broke into wild applause.

Apollo 13 had made it back. The travellers were home from the stars.

Did you know...?

Space accidents

1. The explosion that occurred on Apollo 13 created a cloud in space that was 30 km long. The cloud was so bright that it could easily be seen through telescopes on Earth.

2. Many space flights have come close to disaster. As Apollo 12 blasted off, it was hit by lightning ... twice. The Russian space station, Mir, has suffered a fire, a power failure, and the very first spaceship collision, in its recent accident-prone history.

3. NASA launched its first space station, Skylab, in 1973. Six years later it fell back

into the atmosphere and broke up. Pieces of it came crashing down in the outback of Australia, where, luckily, no one was hit.

4. The worst space accident ever was the Challenger space shuttle disaster. Shortly after lift-off on 28 January 1986, the shuttle exploded, killing all seven crew members.

5. Two woodpeckers once cost NASA $100,000. The pair of pesky birds pecked large holes in a vital part of a space shuttle while it was waiting to be launched.

6. Apollo 16 astronaut Charlie Duke had a nasty surprise during his moonwalk. The drinks holder in his spacesuit went wrong, soaking his hair in cold orange juice.

Astronaut Wanted

Earth orbit – approaching the Mir space station
20 May 1991

I knew that this was the most dangerous part of the whole flight.

Our Soyuz spacecraft was 400 kilometres above the Earth preparing to link with the Mir space station.

"You are go for docking," announced Mission Control.

Since blasting off from Russia, our

Soyuz craft had climbed to the same height as Mir and had gradually moved closer and closer.

The next few minutes were the most important since we left Earth. Any mistake, even the smallest error, by our pilot, and the two space vessels could collide, smashing into each other with disastrous results.

Mission Commander Tolya Artsebarski, the pilot, was sitting next to me as he edged us nearer and nearer to the space station.

I was operating the television cameras that showed Tolya how far away he was from Mir. I had to change from camera to camera at just the right time, so he could see where he was going.

"OK, we're looking good," said Tolya, watching the reading with intense concentration.

"Switching to the wide angle lens," I announced. "It should give you a better view."

He looked over at me with a look that said, "Don't worry, I have done this before you know."

"Stand by. Adjusting entry angle," said Tolya, almost to himself.

There was a reassuring bump and the sudden clang of metal hitting metal.

"We're docked."

"Nice flying," I said.

"Was nothing," said Tolya, with a wicked grin.

We checked that the docking tunnel was airtight, then opened the hatch that now led into Mir.

As the guest cosmonaut, I had the honour of going first. I floated through the connecting tunnel into the large interior of the space station.

"Welcome to Mir!" said Viktor, one of the cosmonauts already on board. He held out some bread and salt – the traditional Russian greeting for new arrivals.

 As I looked around the space station I nearly pinched myself to make sure I was really here...

Two years earlier…

I was driving home on a hot June evening when I first heard the advertisement. I remember being stuck in a traffic jam, listening to the car radio when a voice suddenly caught my attention.

"Astronaut wanted," said the voice. "No experience necessary."

I turned the volume up and listened. The voice went on to say that they were looking for someone aged between 21 and 40, who had a science background, to become Britain's first ever astronaut and travel into space.

 At the end of the advert, the voice gave out a phone number. I grabbed a pen and quickly jotted it down on the back of my hand.

I was 26 years old at the time and had never thought about becoming an astronaut before.

I was working as a scientist at Mars Confectionery, spending my time inventing new kinds of chocolate and ice-cream. It was a great job, always changing, always interesting and I enjoyed it very much.

However, as I drove home, the more I thought about the advertisement the more interested I became. A few days later I gave in to my curiosity and rang the telephone number. A voice told me they'd send me an application form in the next post.

Talk about lazy. When I did receive the form, I have to admit I did nothing with it for a month. It looked long and boring and was going to take a whole evening to fill out.

It was full of those annoying

little questions that you have to think about before you can answer. Suddenly I went off the whole idea: it seemed like a lot of work for nothing.

One evening after work, I found the form lurking menacingly at the bottom of my briefcase. I had had it for so long that I was about to miss the closing date for applications.

Although I expected it to be a total waste of time, I sat down and spent the rest of the night filling it in. The form asked for personal details, what foreign languages I spoke, my level of physical fitness, and if my job in science involved working with my hands as well as my brain.

It took me four hours to complete and the next morning I posted it off with a first class stamp and the word URGENT written in red ink on the envelope.

Two weeks later, the phone in my flat rang. It was very early one morning and I picked it up, only half awake.

"Hello?" I yawned, with my mouth wide open.

"Is that Helen Sharman?"

"Yes, speaking."

"I'm ringing from Air Vice-Marshall Peter Howard's office," said the voice.

I began to wake up rather quickly.

"I'm pleased to tell you that you have been chosen for the first stage of the selection process for the British-Russian Juno Space Mission.

We'd like you to come to London for some medical tests as soon as possible," continued the voice.

Thirteen thousand people had called the same telephone number that I had. Out of those people only 150 had been chosen and it seemed that I was one of them.

Of course I knew that I had no chance of actually being picked, but I thought that it might be interesting to go along and take some of the tests.

I was just an ordinary woman from a very ordinary background. Far too ordinary, I knew, ever to become something exciting like an astronaut.

The first medical tests took place in London. Doctors tested my eyesight, hearing, heartbeat, breathing, and just about anything else they could think of.

They tested my thinking skills with a series of puzzles and

problems I had to solve, racing against the clock to get as many done as possible. It was a bit like being on the longest television quiz show in the world. Endless questions, endless tests.

I found out that before anyone ever gets to fly in space they have to have a huge number of medical tests. Doctors are always looking for any weakness that might stop that person working well in space and therefore endanger the whole mission and other people's lives.

A few weeks after the medicals, I found

out that I had made the shortlist of 32 people. Out of these 32 people, they told me, two would be chosen to go and train in Russia for a year. Out of that pair, one person would be picked to go to the space station.

When I had first sent off my application form, the idea of me actually going into space seemed impossible. Now, however, I was getting more and more excited by the possibility.

I was surprising myself by how much I wanted to be picked.

With the other 31 people, I was invited to attend a series of talks about the mission.

"With the help of the Russians the successful astronaut will visit their space station Mir and spend eight days on board performing scientific experiments," the lecturer informed us.

It was the chance of a lifetime.

I was sure that I would not be chosen. The competition from the other would-be cosmonauts seemed to be too strong.

There were pilots, engineers, skydivers, and even space scientists who all wanted to blast off instead of me.

During the next few months, I became convinced that there was not a single medical test in the world that I had not had – or rather suffered.

The worst test of all took place at an Air Force base in Farnborough. One at a time, we were put into the machine known as the centrifuge.

The centrifuge was a small metal cage

with a single seat inside. The cage was on the end of a giant metal arm that spun it round and round the room at very high speed.

The point of the test was to see how each of us would respond to strong g-forces.

"Looks like a cross between a funfair ride and a torture chamber," I said, as I stepped up for my turn. I found myself being shot round the room like a ball on a pinball table. The only thing I could do was hold on and, most importantly, try not to throw up.

I just about managed it.

When it became time for the people in charge to make their decision, there was nothing I could do except sit and wait. There would be 30 very disappointed people and two winners.

My family and friends had been brilliant, and the people at Mars had really supported me as well. However, I made sure I had told them all that I did not expect to be chosen to go to Moscow. That didn't stop me secretly hoping, though.

A phone call asked me to drive straight down to London for the selection news. At first I was not sure why. Was it to be told that I was no longer needed? When I arrived I was in for a shock.

"Congratulations, Helen! You've made the final two. You and Tim Mace are flying to Moscow to train with the Russian cosmonauts at Star City."

I could not disguise my delight. They'd picked me. *Me!*

When I stepped out of the plane at Moscow Airport a few weeks later, the first things I noticed were the cold and the snow.

Tim and I were taken by bus to Star City, a specially built town where all the Russian cosmonauts live and train.

The first and most important thing that we had to do was to learn to speak Russian. Russian is a very difficult language, not even the letters are the same as in English, but being in Russia helped and we soon began to catch on.

For the next year and a half of our lives, every single day was spent training for the space mission. There were punishing physical workouts in the gym and on the running track as well as lectures on the complex science of space travel. We learned to parachute jump – something that I discovered I loved.

On top of all that, we were taught everything that there was to know about Mir, so that we would be able to cope with any unexpected situations or emergencies that might happen when we were on board.

As the training went on, more and more of our time was spent in the large mock-up of Mir that was at the centre of Star City.

I always trained with two other cosmonauts so I got used to working as part of a close team. I had to learn to rely on other people, just as they would rely on me once we were in space.

After the full 18 months of training, a dreadful decision had to be made. Would it be me or Tim that actually went into space? Although we were now both fully trained cosmonauts, sadly only one of us could visit Mir.

Tim and I had been through a lot together during the long training time and had become good friends. At the same time, we both desperately wanted to be picked.

We were flown back to London to be told the decision there. I was called into the office of Air Vice-Marshall Peter Howard first and nervously took a seat.

"Have you enjoyed your training period?" asked the Air Vice-Marshall.

"Very much," I said. I was in no mood to make small talk. I just wanted to know who had been picked.

"The Commander of Star City says that you and Tim would both make excellent cosmonauts. They would be happy to fly either of you to Mir, so congratulations for that," said the Air Vice-Marshall. "It's a great shame that we have to pick just one of you."

My heart suddenly sank as I realized that he was probably preparing me for bad news.

Then he said, "It was a difficult decision but we've finally decided on you, Helen."

That was it.

 I was going into space.

I was wonderfully happy, but my first thoughts were for Tim.

I knew that he'd be terribly disappointed. It was heartbreaking to have gone through and passed all that training and then not get to fly.

After Tim had been told the decision, I went and had a long talk with him to try and cheer him up. He wished me good luck and gave me a hug.

When I told my family the news they were both scared and thrilled in about equal measures.

I was to be part of a crew of three cosmonauts to be launched on 18 May

1991. A rocket would lift our
small Soyuz spacecraft into orbit
where we would dock with Mir.

I had come so far since hearing that
radio advertisement and jotting down the
number on the back of my hand. I had
travelled half-way around the Earth and
now I was about to leave it completely.

On the morning of our launch, I had
breakfast with the other two cosmonauts –
a long standing tradition in Russian
space travel.

Then, after we were suited up, we climbed
into the bus that would take us to the
launch pad. I caught my breath as the huge
rocket came into sight. I had seen it before,
but today it was taking me into space.

As we drove nearer, I could see that on
the white cone at the very top was the
familiar Russian flag. Next to it someone
had painted, with great care, the Union

Jack – the first time it had
ever appeared on a manned
space mission. I felt
very proud to be
the first Briton
in space.

I boarded the craft with the others and
began my first job, running a series of

safety checks. Every now and
then we could feel the rocket sway
in the strong wind. A reminder
that we were still firmly on Earth.

As the countdown ticked away we had
more than enough last-minute checks to
keep us busy.

Finally, it was time.

"One minute to go. Please close the masks
of your helmets," ordered Mission Control.

"Helmets closed," I responded.

"We are ready to launch," said Mission
Control. "Stand by. Five, four, three, two,
one ... launch!"

Deep below me, I heard a rumbling
noise like distant thunder. It grew louder
and louder as we started to rise from the
launch pad.

I was going into space.

Did you know...?

Animals in space

1. The first living creature to travel into space was a Russian dog called Laika. She orbited the Earth on board Sputnik 2 in 1957.

2. One of the shortest space flights ever was by Hector, a white rat. Hector blasted off from France in 1961 and was sent 160 km into space before landing safe and well just three minutes later.

3. NASA sent two spiders called Arabella and Anita into space to see if they could still spin webs. After some difficulties getting started in the conditions of zero

gravity, their webs were soon as good as usual.

4. An entire colony of honey-bees was launched into space on the American space shuttle in 1984. The hive was closely watched by scientists eager to observe their behaviour.

5. Many unusual animals have been sent into space over the last three decades, including monkeys, mice, flies, ants, frogs, and even a number of jellyfish.

6. In 1990, a quail chick had the honour of becoming the first creature ever born in space when it broke out of its shell on board Mir.

The Eagle has Landed

On board Apollo 11, 360,000 km from Earth
19 July 1969

When Neil Armstrong woke up, he found himself floating in mid-air.

It took him a couple of seconds to remember that he was on his way to the moon. It still seemed unreal, even now as they were flying through space.

Armstrong looked across and saw that his fellow astronauts, Buzz Aldrin and

Mike Collins, were still sleeping soundly.

Armstrong gave himself a push and floated towards the window of the Apollo 11 Command Module. He gazed out at the dark starless void.

"Nothing, but lots of nothing," he said to himself.

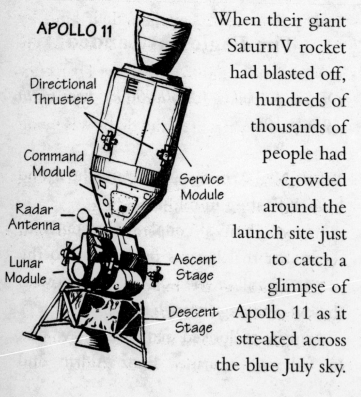

APOLLO 11

Directional Thrusters

Command Module

Radar Antenna

Lunar Module

Service Module

Ascent Stage

Descent Stage

When their giant Saturn V rocket had blasted off, hundreds of thousands of people had crowded around the launch site just to catch a glimpse of Apollo 11 as it streaked across the blue July sky.

Humans were about to walk on the surface of another world for the first time. In countries all over the globe, people were anxiously watching the live television coverage of the mission.

As the three astronauts flew towards the Earth's only natural satellite, their hour by hour progress was carefully followed by millions and millions of people. Thanks to the number of television cameras on board the ship every detail of the flight was being captured live.

The whole world seemed to be holding its breath waiting for the landing.

"Apollo 11, this is Houston. Do you copy?"

The voice on the radio was a wake-up call from Mission Control.

"Roger, Houston," replied Armstrong.

"It's time to rise and shine," said

Mission Control.

"I'll wake the two sleeping beauties over here," volunteered Armstrong, sending a logbook spinning through the zero gravity towards Aldrin's head.

It bumped gently against the sleeping astronaut's forehead.

"Thanks a lot," said Aldrin, floating out of his sleeping-bag with a yawn.

The first order of the day was breakfast. Armstrong took a bite of the tasteless mush that NASA scientists liked to pretend was food.

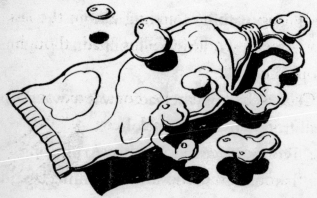

"I told you we should have brought our own burgers and ketchup," said Mike Collins, trying to lighten the mood a little.

Now that the lunar landing was getting closer, all the men could feel a definite tension creeping into the mission.

A manned landing on the moon had been NASA's dream for nearly a decade. The moon was a barren, airless world littered with craters made by ancient meteorite impacts – it was also the Earth's nearest neighbour in space.

There were a hundred things that could go wrong with the landing and in the last few weeks, Mike Collins had thought about them all.

Collins had what he considered to be the easy job. He would keep the Command Module in orbit around the moon, while

Armstrong and Aldrin used the Lunar Module to fly down and land on the surface.

Although he had said nothing to his friends, Collins was far from confident about their chances of success. They could crash on landing, run out of fuel, or worse.

Perhaps Collins's greatest fear was an engine failure that would leave his shipmates stranded on the moon for ever. If it happened there would be nothing he could do to help them, no matter how much he wanted to.

They had finished breakfast now and were clearing away the empty packets and the few crumbs that floated around inside the ship.

"Buzz and I are going to check out all our equipment for tomorrow," said Armstrong.

His tone was so matter of fact, that he could have been talking about going on a camping trip instead of landing on the moon.

"I think things are going pretty well," said Collins, doing his best to sound as confident as his commander. "If things go as well tomorrow, we should be OK."

The spaceship was suddenly plunged into near darkness.

"Hey, who turned out the sun?" asked Aldrin.

The men floated to the cabin windows and looked out. The warming glow of the yellow sun was gone. They had just flown into the moon's shadow.

"Look at those stars!" whispered Collins.

The blackness of space was suddenly full of gleaming red, white and blue stars. They looked so bright and so clear that you could almost taste them.

"What the astronomers on Earth would give to see this," said Aldrin.

Then Aldrin saw that Armstrong was not listening. He wasn't even looking at the stars.

Armstrong's gaze was focused straight down towards the rocky surface of the moon. His eyes wrinkled slightly as he studied the mountains, canyons and craters passing under the ship.

Aldrin suddenly realized what his commander was doing. He was looking for a place to land.

"Let's get this show on the road," said Armstrong.

He flicked the final row of switches and brought the Lunar Module, called Eagle, humming into life.

"We have engine ignition," confirmed Aldrin, sitting next to him in the tiny ship.

Back on Earth, people were gathering around their televisions. In Japan, there had been such a pre-landing rush to buy sets that the shops had sold out.

In America, people were planning to hold moonwalk parties to celebrate the landing. Altogether 600 million people around the world were watching a unique piece of history.

In space, Mike Collins watched through

the window of the Command Module as the two ships separated.

"You guys take it easy on the moonwalk. No huffing and puffing around, OK?" called Collins, over the radio link.

At the controls of the Lunar Module, Armstrong used a short burst of thruster fire to start the ship moving.

"You're looking good," said Collins as he watched the spider-like craft disappearing into the distance. "You guys take care."

"See you later," said Armstrong, flatly. All his concentration and energy now was going into flying the Lunar Module.

"Ten thousand metres," said Aldrin, noting their height above the lunar surface. It was Aldrin's job to call out the details of their flight, so that Armstrong knew exactly where they were. At the moment, the on-board computer had control of the ship. The plan was to let the computer fly the Lunar Module down to a height of around 200 metres. Then Armstrong would take over manual control and guide the ship down to a safe landing site.

"Five thousand metres," reported Aldrin. Armstrong checked that the Lunar Module's camera was switched on and sending pictures back to Earth. He didn't want the people back home to miss this. Armstrong leaned forward and fired up the descent engine which would slow their fall towards the area of the moon known as the Sea of Tranquillity.

"Engine working."

"And right on time," added Aldrin.

They were closer to the moon now and Armstrong began scanning the surface, looking for a place they could land.

As he studied the strange landscape of craters and canyons below him, the ship lurched from side to side as the computer automatically fired the thrusters. It was starting to be a bumpy ride.

"One thousand metres."

"Beeeeeeeep."

"What's that?" said Armstrong, clearly worried.

A loud alarm sounded in the ship. Aldrin's heart missed a beat as he realized that they might have to abandon the landing.

"Houston, we have an alarm signal. Can you tell us what's wrong?" asked Aldrin.

"Roger, Eagle. The alarm is sounding

because your computer is being over-worked. Don't worry. Ignore it. You are still go for landing," ordered the voice of Mission Control.

Eagle was now only 200 metres above the moon's surface.

Armstrong looked down and saw with alarm that the Lunar Module was heading straight towards a large crater.

If the computer tried to land there, it would be a disaster.

"The computer is taking us into a crater. I'm going to have to take over control," said Armstrong.

They had a limited amount of fuel and Armstrong knew that they needed to land soon.

"One hundred metres," reported Aldrin.

Armstrong used the thrusters to slow their descent even more and the Lunar Module passed over the hostile looking crater.

On the other side of the crater, a series of large boulders came into view. There was still nowhere to land.

"How's the fuel lasting?" asked Armstrong.

"We've got about two minutes left," said Aldrin.

"I'm going to land us over there," decided Armstrong, suddenly spotting an area of flat ground. Back at Houston, the controllers and scientists knew that Armstrong had already switched to manual control.

There was nothing more they could say or do. The success or failure of the entire space programme now rested in the hands of one man.

"Seventy-five metres."

"No, wait. There's another crater. That area's no good either. We'll have to get over it."

Every second that passed, precious fuel was wasted.

As Eagle cleared the second crater, Armstrong caught sight of a large flat piece of land. It looked perfect for a landing.

"Thirty metres."

They were so close now that the Lunar Module's engine began to blow up a thick cloud of moon dust.

"I can't see the surface any more. We're stirring up too much dust," said Armstrong.

Below him, the moon suddenly looked like it was covered with a thick blanket of fog. The surface that he had just been watching had now disappeared.

"I'm going in."

"Ten metres."

Back in Houston, no one was talking. No one was even breathing.

All over the world, families sat huddled together in edgy silence, staring at their television screens. All they could do was watch the flickering images being beamed at them from another world and hope.

The man at the centre of it all, Neil Armstrong, adjusted the thrusters once more and a blast of dust hit the windows.

The Lunar Module sank slowly towards the surface and landed with the gentlest of bumps.

"Contact," said Armstrong.

He quickly switched off the engine and the two astronauts grinned at each other.

"Houston, this is Tranquillity Base here. The Eagle has landed."

In Mission Control, it took several long minutes for the

cheers and applause to die down.

They had done it.

The Lunar
Module stood
completely
alone in the
Sea of
Tranquillity.
  Apollo 11
had landed
near the
southern edge
of the Sea of
Tranquillity,
a flat lowland
on the moon's
eastern half.

Inside the Lunar Module, the two astronauts helped each other put on their spacesuits. Aldrin strapped on his companion's backpack containing his air supply.

"Am I hooked up right?"

"Your oxygen supply is working fine."

With their gloves and space helmets in place, it was time to open the outer hatch and step out.

It took two attempts before the metal door finally moved.

Neil Armstrong carefully eased his now-bulky form through the small opening. He began gently to lower himself down the Lunar Module's ladder. "From up here, the surface looks like a fine yellow powder," said Armstrong, excitement creeping into his voice.

He got ready to step off the ladder.

Neil Armstrong knew that the first words spoken on the moon would go down in history. He had not known what he was going to say until just a few minutes ago, but now he was certain.

"That's one small step for man," he said as his boot touched the surface, "one giant leap for mankind."

He let go of the ship's ladder and walked away from the Lunar Module with a strange slow-motion bounce.

Mankind was on the moon.

A few moments later, Buzz Aldrin joined him on the surface. He gazed around at the rocks and craters that stretched as far as the eye could see.

"Beautiful."

"Isn't it something?" agreed Armstrong.

After all their training and planning, nothing had prepared them for the actual moon itself.

As they looked around they saw that they had touched down on a wide plain. There were rocks and sharp boulders lying around and a number of craters dented the surface.

Beneath their moon boots, the surface seemed to be covered in a layer of dust a few centimetres thick, with a rocky surface underneath it.

The sky above them was black, with the Earth shining like a blue jewel.

"We're a long way from home," said Armstrong, quietly.

The two astronauts began working through the list of mission tasks that Mission Control had set them.

First they gathered as many samples of different moon rocks as they could find.

When they had finished, Armstrong threw away the hammer he had used with a casual, almost lazy toss.

The hammer flew away from him, spinning round and round in a slow graceful motion. It finally hit the surface 80 metres away and sent up a spray of fine moon dust.

The next hour was spent setting up two different sets of experiments that they would leave on the moon's surface. As well as all that they also found time to plant a flag-pole and fly the American flag.

By the time the men had finished, the area around the Lunar Module was covered with their footprints. Footprints that, without any atmosphere, without any wind or rain, would stay exactly the same for millions of years after they had left.

When the men climbed back inside the

Lunar Module nearly three hours later and took off their helmets, the first thing they noticed was the smell of the moon dust on their spacesuits.

"Kinda like gunpowder," said Aldrin.

"Or a fire cracker when it's just exploded," agreed Armstrong.

There was one final test to come. Now they had to leave the moon and get home again.

If, for any reason, the engine failed to work then there would be little they could do except sit and wait for their oxygen to run out.

Armstrong pushed the button that began the two minute countdown to blast off.

"Beginning countdown sequence," said Armstrong. "Keep your fingers crossed."

Both men knew that this was their

last big hurdle between them and a safe return to Earth ... and their families.

"Five, four, three, two, one ... zero."

For just a second nothing happened at all. Then the men felt their stomachs lurch as the Lunar Module began to rise from the surface.

Outside, the Lunar Module's engine exhaust blew over the flag-pole, sending it falling into the moon dust.

"There he is!" smiled Aldrin.

In the distance above them he could already see the Command Module waiting for their return. Once they redocked and were inside, then they could really begin the journey home.

They were returning to a world that had changed since their departure. A world that had been united and utterly captivated by the adventures of three explorers far from home.

Humankind had taken its first fragile steps into space. And there were footprints all over the moon to prove it.

Did you know...?

The moon

1. When the crew of Apollo 11 returned to Earth they were forced to stay in a special area all alone for the first two weeks in case they had brought back any "moon germs".

2. The first man on the moon, Neil Armstrong, was flying mad. He began taking flying lessons when he was just 14. By 16 he had got his official pilot's licence.

3. On the way to the moon, Buzz Aldrin reported seeing strange flashes of light. His crewmates thought he was imagining it, but later the flashes were discovered to be cosmic

rays passing through the astronaut's eyes.

4. There is a mirror on the surface of the moon. It was left there by Armstrong and Aldrin during their moonwalk. Scientists on Earth can fire a laser at the mirror, which reflects the light back and lets them measure exactly how far away the moon is.

5. On later moon missions, the astronauts drove a lunar buggy which worked on electricity. It allowed the astronauts to explore much further from base than if they had to walk everywhere on foot.

6. The moon is gradually moving away from the Earth... at the cosmic rate of two millimetres a month.